Collins Scottish H

MARY QUEEN OF SCOTS AND THE SCOTTISH REFORMATION

1540–1587

Sydney Wood

Collins Educational

An Imprint of HarperCollins*Publishers*

Published by Collins Educational
An imprint of HarperCollins *Publishers* Ltd
77–85 Fulham Palace Road
Hammersmith
London W6 8JB

The HarperCollins website is:
www.**fire**and**water**.com

© HarperCollins *Publishers* Ltd 1999

First published 1999

ISBN 000327129 3

Sydney Wood asserts the moral right to be identified as the author of this work.

British Library Cataloguing in Publication Data
A catalogue record for this publication is available from the British Library.

Acknowledgements
p.6: (Mary being forced to abdicate)
 Mary Evans Picture Library
p.7: (the ruins of Melrose Abbey by John Slezar)
 The National Library of Scotland, Edinburgh
p.8: (view of Dundee by John Slezar)
 Trustees of the National Library of Scotland, Edinburgh
p.10: ('The Shoemaker' The Book of Trades)
 Trustees of the National Library of Scotland, Edinburgh
p.17: (view of Stirling Castle by John Slezar)
 Trustees of the National Library of Scotland, Edinburgh
p.19: (engraving of John Knox after a portrait by Adrian Vanson)
 Scottish National Portrait Gallery
p.22: (Mary Stuart, Queen of Scots
 Courtesy of 'Historical Personalities'
 (Holyrood House)
 The Royal Collection © Her Majesty the Queen
p.24: (John Knox lecturing Mary Stuart, by Samuel Sidley)
 Towneley Hall Art Gallery and Museum, Burnley/The Bridgeman Art Library
p.25: (Henry Darnley and Mary Stuart, the King and Queen of Scots)
 Courtesy of the National Trust
p.28: (The murder of Rizzio, by Sir William Allan)
 National Gallery of Scotland
 (Kirk O'Field MPF 366)
 Public Record Office Image Library
p.31: (Lochleven Castle)
 Edinburgh Photographic Library
p.36: (Execution of Mary Queen of Scots by an unknown Dutch artist)
 Scottish National Portrait Gallery
p.38: (portrait of James Stuart as a child)
 National Galleries of Scotland
p.39: (portrait of James Douglas, Earl of Morton)
 Courtesy of 'Historical Personalities'

Edited by Joanne Stone
Design by Derek Lee
Map artwork by Chartwell Illustrators
Illustrations by Mary McKenna
Production by Anna Pauletti
Printed by Scotprint, Musselburgh

Contents

Timeline

1538	King James V of Scotland marries a French noblewoman, Mary of Guise.
1542	Birth of Princess Mary. The Scots are heavily defeated by the English army at Solway Moss. James V dies. Mary becomes Queen but has a Regent to rule for her until she grows up.
1543	**Treaty of Greenwich**: Mary to marry Henry VIII's young son, Edward. Scottish Parliament rejects treaty.
1544	English forces begin attacks on Scottish borders.
1546	George Wishart is burned to death for being a Protestant. Protestant Fife lairds seize St Andrews Castle and murder the Catholic Cardinal Beaton.
1547	French forces take St Andrews Castle. The English army defeats the Scots at the Battle of Pinkie.
1548	**Treaty of Haddington**: Mary to marry Francis, the heir to the French throne.
1554	Mary of Guise becomes Regent.
1557	First gathering of Scottish Protestant Lords of the Congregation.
1558	Mary marries Francis. Henry VIII's daughter Elizabeth becomes Queen of England.
1559	John Knox returns to Scotland. Riots by Protestants in Perth. Several burghs appoint Protestant ministers.
1560	English forces support Protestant Scots. Mary of Guise dies. **Treaty of Edinburgh**: French and English forces withdraw. Mary is widowed. The Scottish Parliament bans the celebration of Mass.
1561	Mary returns to Scotland.
1565	She marries Darnley.
1566	The murder of Rizzio. Mary's son James is born.
1567	The murder of Darnley. Mary marries Earl of Bothwell. Mary's supporters are defeated at Carberry Hill. Mary is imprisoned and forced to abdicate. Her son becomes King James VI, and the Earl of Moray becomes Regent.
1568	Mary and her army are defeated at Langside. She escapes to England.
1570	Moray is killed.
1572	John Knox dies. The Earl of Morton becomes Regent.
1574	Andrew Melville returns to Scotland.
1581	The Earl of Morton is executed.
1582	'Ruthven Raid': King James is kidnapped.
1583	King James escapes.
1584	The 'Black Acts' declare that the King is supreme in Church affairs.
1586	Babington Plot to kill Elizabeth. Mary is found guilty of involvement.
1587	Mary is executed.

Introduction

This book deals with events that happened more than 400 years ago. It deals with a time of conflict, trouble and tragedy. Yet what happened in these years powerfully shaped life in Scotland in ways that still affect us today. Events of these years changed people's religious beliefs. They also altered the way that many Scots thought about England. They paved the way for a Scot to become the King of England.

This book is divided into six main chapters:

■ *1 The Queen's Scotland* considers **what Scotland was like** in the early sixteenth century, including how the country was ruled.

■ *2 Troubled Times* deals with the crisis caused by both the **death of the King** and the **growth of Protestantism** which challenged the existing Church.

■ *3 Mary's Rule* deals with **Queen Mary's return to Scotland** from France, and how she ruled.

■ *4 Murders, Mysteries and Exile* deals with the **troubles that beset Mary** and how they led to her being forced to abdicate and then to leave Scotland.

■ *5 Mary's Last Years* deals with the **sad end of Mary's life** in exile in England.

■ *6 Regents and Reformation* deals with how the Regents ruled while James VI was very young, how a different kind of Scottish Church was set up, and **how James ruled in the early years** of his reign. Finally, the *Postscript* looks at how Mary has been remembered over the centuries and is remembered today.

Certain themes run through the book. Key themes to think about are:

The Church:

Religion played a very important part in everybody's life. What was it like? How did it change?

The Crown:

How did the Queen try to rule? What happened when there wasn't a responsible adult to be King or Queen?

Authority:

Who had real power in Scotland at this time? Did this change in any way? If so, why?

This is a history book. It provides both knowledge and understanding of the past and insights into how we know about the past in several ways.

Information

This comes in:
- Brief lists of key points
- Text
- Diagrams
- Maps
- Some illustrations

Sources of historical evidence

These may be:
- Views about the past written many years ago
- Historians' views
- Drawings and paintings from the past
- Old buildings
- Illustrations

There are activities in the book to test and develop your historical skills. Can you:

- Show your knowledge and understanding of historical developments, events and issues using knowledge that is relevant and accurate?

- Explain historical developments and events in an organised way using accurate and relevant information?

- Evaluate historical sources showing that you have thought about:
  - their origin or purpose?
  - their content?
  - their context?
  - comparisons between sources?

In each chapter you will find questions to help you think about what you have read.

STOP AND THINK

STOP AND THINK *Raises questions for you to discuss*

At the end of each chapter is a section for you to practise your skills, with questions based on primary sources which need a more detailed response. Throughout the book the question is raised of how reliable the historical sources are.

The picture on the left shows Mary Queen of Scots being forced to abdicate. It is an engraving of a painting by Sir William Allan from the late 19th century, so … ***Is it accurate?***

What questions would you want to answer before accepting this as an accurate or helpful source?

This is an important matter to think about. Not many sources have survived from the actual time of Mary Queen of Scot. ***What is safe to trust?***

The Queen's Country

Key Points
This chapter deals with:
- Life in the countryside.
- Life in burghs.
- The Catholic Church in Scotland.
- The people who ruled Scotland.

Mary Stuart, Queen of Scots

On 8 December 1542, King James V of Scotland lay dying in his royal palace at Falkland. His servants brought him a message from Linlithgow Palace that his Queen, Mary of Guise (a French noblewoman), had just given birth to Scotland's next ruler. The King listened sadly to the news that the baby was a girl. It seemed to him that his family, the Stuarts, who had once gained the crown through marriage to Robert the Bruce's daughter, would now lose it. He murmured:

It cam' wi' a lass and it will gang wi' a lass.

How could a girl rule Scotland in such troubled times? The King's army had just been heavily defeated at Solway Moss by an English army that might well launch further attacks. James lived just a few more days, dying at about midnight on 14 December. His daughter Mary, who was just six days old, was now Queen.

Scotland in 1542

What was Scotland like at this time? How might a Scot of the time have described it to a visitor from another country?

This drawing comes from a seventeenth-century book written and illustrated by John Slezar, a German who worked for the Scottish King. Read the following sections and consider what the man on the left might be explaining about Scotland to the woman who is, perhaps, coming to the country for the first time.

The countryside

◆ BURGHS – larger place often local centres for merchants and craftsmen

◆ TOWNSHIPS – places larger than a village but smaller and more rural than a burgh

Most of Scotland's half-million inhabitants lived in the countryside. Just 2 per cent lived in the larger BURGHS. Their lives were full of dangers, the first being the struggle to survive early childhood. Their average life expectancy was just 30 years.

Most people lived in little clusters of houses called TOWNSHIPS. A seventeenth-century English visitor to Scotland described what many of these homes were like:

The walls are made of a few stones jumbled together without mortar to cement them. On them they put pieces of wood meeting at the top, ridge fashion. They cover these houses with turf an inch thick. It is rare to find chimneys – a small hole in the roof carries away the smoke.

◆ RIG – mound of soil wide enough for a plough to go down its length

These homes also did not have windows. Around the houses stretched unfenced farmland with soil piled up in great long mounds called 'RIGS'. Each rig was wide enough for a plough to go down its length. Crops of oats and barley grew on top of these mounds and Scotland's frequent rains drained off them into the hollows between them. Cabbages, peas and beans, were also part of the Scots' diet. Hens and pigs were kept too, along with a few cows for milking. The local people used their skills to construct houses and furniture, and make clothes, shoes and the rest of life's necessities.

The local landowner controlled the lives of people in the townships. They had to pay him rent, supply animals to pull his plough and take their corn to his mill to be ground. Sometimes the younger men even had to go with their local lord to fight for him in battle. Women, too, faced a life of endless work. They could marry from the age of twelve, though most married in their twenties. They were expected to have several children (since few of them would survive because infant death was so common). Women had to care for the family, help with farm work, make and mend clothes, fetch water and fuel, and prepare food over open fires.

The burghs

Although most people lived in the countryside, there was a growing number of different-sized burghs where a large number of people lived, crowded together. Some burghs had just a few hundred inhabitants, others were bigger and housed several thousand. This drawing of Dundee was made in the seventeenth century but it gives an idea of what one of these bigger burghs looked like.

Some burghs were set up by the Church, while Scottish Kings created royal burghs. Important landowners also set up places

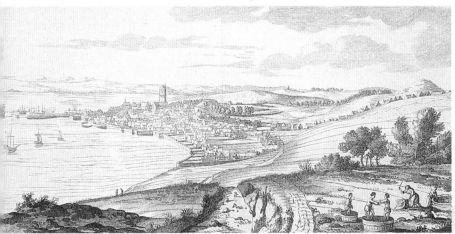

Dundee around 1680

The Scottish burghs in 1542.

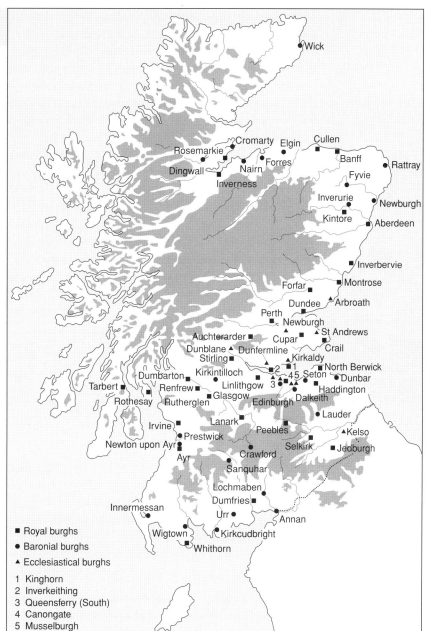

■ Royal burghs
● Baronial burghs
▲ Ecclesiastical burghs

1 Kinghorn
2 Inverkeithing
3 Queensferry (South)
4 Canongate
5 Musselburgh

called burghs of barony. The map shows where these burghs were at the time of Mary's birth.

Look carefully at both the drawing of Dundee and the map of the burghs in Scotland. Why were burghs set up in these types of location?

Burghs were centres for craftsmen and for traders. Only royal burghs enjoyed the privilege of trading with overseas countries. Scotland exported mainly raw materials like wool, skins, fish, salt and coal. Imports were often luxury or manufactured goods such as fine wines and cloth. Travel at this time was extremely difficult because the

◆ WRIGHTS – men who made things from wood or metal, e.g. cartwright and ship-wright

◆ DEACON – leader of a craftsman's guild

roads were very poor and there were few bridges. Burghs were usually set up by the sea or a river so that goods could be transported by water.

In burghs you could find craftsmen such as shoemakers, tailors, masons, saddlers, WRIGHTS, skinners, bakers, candle makers, weavers and brewers. They usually worked by hand, using simple tools. Men learned their trade by being apprenticed for seven years to master craftsmen. The crafts were organised into guilds. Each guild had a leader (a DEACON) who checked that apprentices were properly trained and that goods offered for sale were of good quality and fairly priced.

Goods were sold from the craftsmen's workplace and in an open market area where there was usually a market cross. Local trade flourished around the marketplace and was sternly controlled by the burgh leaders, the BURGESSES. These men had to be wealthy enough to afford the fee required to become a burgess and so were drawn from the ranks of successful merchants and craftsmen. They enjoyed all sorts of privileges, such as being served before other people.

Traders who were not from the burgh could only do business with the burgesses' permission and had to pay for this privilege. The town council was made up of burgesses and they made laws for their burgh, like this one from the sixteenth century:

A sixteenth-century shoemaker.

It is ordered by the council of Glasgow that there be no dearer ale sold than sixpence a pint and that the ale be good. And that no one brews it except FREEMEN or the widows of freemen. And that the fourpenny loaf weighs eight ounces. And that the deacon of the craft inspect the bread and if the baker is found to be negligent, he be punished.

Houses in burghs were crammed close together. The streets did not have proper drains or sewers and every sort of rubbish was dumped in them. The streets were foul-smelling and diseases spread quickly. In the 1530s Edinburgh was hit by plague, a disease carried by rat fleas which spread easily in burghs.

Beggars from around Scotland crowded into burghs too. Many councils passed laws against them, like this one in Dundee (1556) which declared:

◆ BURGESSES – important men in the burghs

◆ FREEMAN – a man who enjoyed all the rights and privileges of living in a burgh

No beggars be found in this town but they were born here and that are too feeble, weak, or old to work. If they are not old and of the burgh and still beg, they will be burned on the cheek and banished.

Religion in Scotland

◆ REFORMATION – the name given to the split between Catholics and those who followed the ideas of reformers like Martin Luther (Protestants)

At the time of Mary's birth in 1542, most of the people of Scotland were Roman Catholics, but a number were becoming interested in the Protestant beliefs of a German monk, Martin Luther. In 1517, he put forward a long list of criticisms of the Catholic Church. His ideas spread in Germany and Switzerland in a movement called 'the REFORMATION'. Several Scots went to the continent to study the ideas of the Protestant reformers. They were especially interested in the beliefs of John Calvin – a reformer who had set up his own religious community in Switzerland.

◆ HERETICS – people who believed religious ideas that were dangerously wrong

The Pope and the Catholic Church condemned people like Luther and Calvin as HERETICS. Protestants wished to end the Pope's authority. Calvinists wanted to go even further and abolish bishops and the whole power structure of the Church.

Protestants also believed that everybody should be able to read the Bible, which was written in Latin – a language only churchmen and a few others could read. William Tyndale translated the Bible's New Testament into English in 1525, so that people could read the Bible themselves. This helped to spread Protestant beliefs.

King James V had done his best to protect the Catholic Church in Scotland from Protestant ideas but a bitter conflict between Catholics and Protestants began to develop. Each side was keen to have the backing of their local lord or landowner so that force could be used on their behalf.

The problems of the Catholic Church

Some people criticised the Catholic Church in Scotland because:

■ The Catholic Church was wealthy.

■ Some churchmen lived very comfortable lives while ordinary people worked hard.

■ Some monks and nuns did not keep their vows to live very holy lives.

■ Kings used their power to provide their children with Church positions. James IV's son became Archbishop of St Andrews when he was just eleven years old, and four of James V's illegitimate sons were also given Church positions though technically they were at least clergy.

■ Some churchmen were PLURALISTS so they couldn't do all their work properly.

◆ PLURALIST – someone holding several church posts at one time

◆ COMMENDATOR – protector of a church or abbey who had control of its income

■ Many parishes had their funds reduced by cathedrals, abbeys and universities to fund new church buildings. This left local priests in need of income. So they charged the people in their parishes for special services such as a christening, a ceremony no parent would dare let their child go without.

■ Some nobles who had managed to secure the post of 'COMMENDATOR' (protector) of a church or abbey for themselves through their power and influence got control of its income. They paid someone else a small wage to do the work.

■ Attempts to reform the Church were not sufficiently successful.

The Scottish Parliament tried to bring about improvements with laws like this one from 1542:

> *Because of the neglect of the Divine Service and also the dishonesty and misbehaviour of churchmen in such matters as knowledge and manners, so that churchmen are despised; the King encourages all churchmen to reform themselves and everyone under their control.*

Perhaps Scots were coming to expect more from their churchmen. Certainly they enjoyed seeing an entertainment intending to ridicule the Church written by Sir David Lindsay in 1541. In this piece an abbot says:

My mistress is both as fat and fair as any wench inside the town of Ayr. I send my sons to Paris to the school; I trust in God that they will not be fools. And all my daughters I have well provided. Now judge yourselves if I am not well guided.

STOP AND THINK

Why were some Scots dissatisfied with the Catholic Church in Scotland?

How Scotland was ruled

The monarch

The monarch personally directed the Scottish government. It was vital for peace and good order that the monarch was hardworking, a good leader, and able to manage the nobles. However, the monarch did have some help:

- The Privy Council offered advice. It included nobles and hardworking lawyers who were able to help the monarch and run business affairs.

- Parliament met once or twice a year to discuss and pass laws. Parliament was made up of nobles, important churchmen and representatives of the royal burghs. It was not elected by ordinary people.

- The College of Justice was set up by James V to try to develop law and order in Scotland.

- The monarch's army was quite small. When he needed a large army, he called on his nobles to bring their own men.

Personal rule meant that Scottish government was not costly. There were few taxes. The monarch lived on an income from royal burghs and lands. However, there were some problems with this method of government, as a French visitor, Jean de Beaugue, noticed:

When at war the Scots are likely to have to live at their own expense and bring what they need. During this time they try to meet the enemy, and fight in a very determined way (especially against the English whom they hate because they are neighbours and cause jealousy). Once they've eaten all their food they break camp or withdraw.

A monarch had to be a strong ruler. James V, Mary's father, had been determined to suppress any opposition to him. He had executed James Hamilton, a leading noble, and put other nobles in prison. The Earl of Angus escaped James's anger by fleeing to England. James had also attacked the troublesome Borders area and executed James Armstrong, one of the local leaders. Yet if a monarch were too forceful, and turned nobles against him, it could lessen his authority. James's military disaster at Solway Moss in 1542 was partly because many nobles were reluctant to help him.

The nobles

There were many nobles and lords in Scotland. There was often great rivalry between them, and jealousy of any noble who seemed to be becoming too powerful. John Major, a Scot of the time, wrote:

> *If two nobles of equal rank happen to be very near neighbours, quarrels and even shedding of blood are a common thing between them.*

The support of nobles was essential for a monarch to rule properly. Scotland was a difficult country to travel round, with the Highlands being a particular problem. Monarchs needed local lords to rule the regions for them. When war broke out, they needed these nobles to bring men to fight.

When Scotland did not have an adult monarch, nobles struggled with one another for control of the country. Sometimes they looked for help from abroad – especially from France and England.

Nobles gathered relatives and lesser lords around them. In return for their support, great nobles took care of their friends and relations. Members of the Gordon family, for example, gathered around their leader, the Earl of Huntly, and prospered when he prospered.

Local lords controlled the lives of the ordinary Scots. They rented land to the Scots to farm. The monarch often appointed them as the local sheriffs, and the lords' local courts could try every offence except treason.

STOP AND THINK

How easy might it be for a girl like Mary to rule Scotland?

Scotland in the 1540s was a dangerous place. Men carried swords and daggers. Nobles surrounded themselves with armed men. Quarrels between Catholics and Protestants were added to the endless struggles for power and wealth. Mary was the only legitimate monarch but her father had several illegitimate children too – seven boys and two girls in total. Several boys were placed in church posts but Mary's older half-brother, James Stuart (later Earl of Moray), was a Protestant and had ambitions of his own.

Practise Your Skills

Answer the question that follows, using the sources and your knowledge as appropriate.

Source A, from the writings of the historian T. C. Smout:

'The Scottish [Catholic] Church had long been remarkable for its corruption. Except in Perth ... the Scottish monasteries had by 1559 long since ceased to be the [means] of spirituality. James V had [got] permission from the Pope ... to appoint 3 baby sons, all illegitimate, to be abbots of Kelso and Montrose, priors of St Andrews and Pittenweem and abbot of Holyrood.'

Source B, from the writings of the historian Michael Lynch:

'Scottish monasteries seem to have largely escaped the worst moral vices ... there were signs that the traditional devotions were flourishing in many houses [monasteries] ... young men were flowing into the monasteries in the 1550s ... if there was a monastic crisis it was one of economics rather than spirituality [for they] were more vulnerable than most to the continuing decline in the wool trade. The century before the Reformation was, in one sense, a period of achievement for the Church. Three university colleges were founded and vast sums were expended by towns people on the erection of their churches.'

1 In what ways do the views in Sources A and B differ from one another? (Evaluate historical sources taking into account origin or purpose and context.)

Chapter 1: An overview

Ordinary people

- Most ordinary people lived in the countryside, farming together, living a very hard life in miserable conditions. They paid rent to their local landowner and carried out duties for him.
- Some lived in burghs where there were craftsmen and merchants. Burghs helped provide wealth for Scotland. Burgesses had special privileges.

The ruling class

James V's death left a baby girl to become Queen at a time when a strong monarch was needed. There were two powerful groups in the kingdom which helped to run the government, the Church and the nobles.

- Some people had started to criticise the **Church**.
- Support of **the nobles** was essential for the peaceful ruling of Scotland.

Troubled Times

Key Points
This chapter deals with:
- The struggle between different people to gain control of Scotland.
- English attacks on Scotland.
- French involvement in Scotland.
- The growth of Protestantism.

The struggle for power

Mary was born in 1542. It was 1561 before she took control as Queen. During these years Scotland lived through very troubled times. Without a strong ruler's leadership, various important people and foreign countries tried to gain control.

Mary of Guise, the Queen's French Catholic mother, wanted to rule the country.

Powerful nobles like the Douglas family, the Hamilton family and the Gordon family, wanted wealth and power.

France wanted to help Mary of Guise and her Scottish supporters control Scotland since this helped France during its quarrels with England.

England wanted its Scottish supporters to be in charge since this kept the northern frontier peaceful.

The growing number of Protestants wanted to destroy the power of the Catholic Church in Scotland and needed control of the country to do this.

Scotland

England

France

These struggles resulted in a time of trouble. Foreign ships and soldiers (both French and English) came to Scotland. Scottish nobles tried to decide which was the better side to support. Battles were fought, and people burned crops and buildings – including many religious ones. Yet for most of this troubled time the young Queen was not in Scotland.

'The Rough Wooing'

As the Queen was an infant, James Hamilton, Earl of Arran, was made the supreme Governor of Scotland. He was not a very forceful or decisive man, and found that he was endlessly pushed and pulled by other people. Mary of Guise and Cardinal David Beaton, the Archbishop of St Andrews, wanted Scotland to remain Catholic and pro-French. King Henry VIII of England had other ideas. He saw a marriage between his five-year-old son Edward and the infant Mary as the ideal way of making sure that Scotland would, in future, be England's friend. For the moment, Arran was persuaded to agree with Henry.

The Treaty of Greenwich, 1 July 1543

This stated that the Mary and Edward would marry. Meanwhile, an English noble and his wife would come to Scotland to keep an eye on Mary and her education as she grew up. But Arran found that news of this Treaty stirred anger in Scotland. Henry made this worse by his behaviour. He demanded an end to Scotland's alliance with France, made it clear that he thought Mary should move to England, and seized several Scottish ships. In December, the Scottish Parliament rejected the Treaty, using the excuse that Henry had not bothered to formally agree it. Arran was now much more influenced by Beaton, Mary of Guise and all those who disliked both Henry's interference and his religion (because Henry had ended the Pope's power in England and made himself head of the Church of England).

Henry was furious. He sent the Earl of Hertford with an army to attack Scotland, saying:

> *Put all to fire and the sword. Burn Edinburgh and so destroy it that it will remain a memory of the vengeance of God upon the Scots for their falsehood and disobedience.*

Hertford obeyed his orders. English armies launched repeated attacks, destroying part of Edinburgh, burning crops and wrecking abbeys in the Borders such as Melrose and Jedburgh. This violent campaign has been given the title 'The Rough Wooing'.

Scottish forces did win a success at Ancrum Moor, but, overall, the campaigns brought repeated setbacks. Encouraged by Henry VIII, a group of Protestant Fife lairds captured St Andrews Castle and murdered Cardinal Beaton. Even Henry VIII's death in January 1547 did not end the onslaughts. Hertford became Duke of Somerset and Lord Protector while Edward VI was too young to rule (in the same way that Arran was Governor). He launched fresh attacks, and won a big victory at Pinkie in which as many as 10,000 Scots were killed. English troops occupied strong points on the Border and up the East Coast. An English base was set up in Haddington. A fresh English army moved north to begin a new campaign.

Rescue by the French?

Small groups of French forces began to help the Scots. A French force took St Andrews Castle from the pro-English Scottish Protestants who had murdered Cardinal Beaton and taken the castle. The new French King, Henry II, now proposed an alliance which Scottish leaders had to accept as the only way of avoiding defeat by Somerset.

The Treaty of Haddington, 7 July 1548

Scottish and French leaders agreed that:

- The King's eldest son, Francis, would marry Mary.

- Mary was to go to France.

- French forces would stop the English advance.

Stirling Castle where Mary was crowned.

Mary's safety had long been a worry. She had first been taken from Linlithgow to Stirling Castle where, at nine months old, she was crowned Queen. Then she was sent to Inchmahome Priory and then, in 1548, to Dumbarton Castle. The fear that she might be kidnapped by English agents, or their Scottish Protestant friends, remained. Arran and Mary of Guise agreed that the little girl should go to France. In return, a huge fleet of more than 100 French ships arrived. Somerset was distracted by other problems in England, making it easier for French forces to push his troops out of Scotland, and a peace treaty was eventually signed. Long before peace arrived, Mary left Dumbarton on 7 August 1548 aboard a ship bound for France. With her went four attendants, Mary Seton, Mary Beaton, Mary Fleming and Mary Livingstone (the four Marys). The six-day voyage was a troubled one, and at one point violent seas broke the rudder of the ship. Mary, however, remained well and cheerful when all around her were ill.

The next 13 years may well have been the most carefree of Mary's life. She grew into a tall, strong and handsome young woman who loved dancing, riding, hunting and gossiping with friends. A French courtier noted:

> *So graceful was her French that the judgement of the most learned men recognised her command of the language. Nor did she neglect Spanish or Italian. She followed Latin more readily than she spoke it. Her excellence in singing comes from a natural ability. The instruments she played were the harp and harpsichord.*

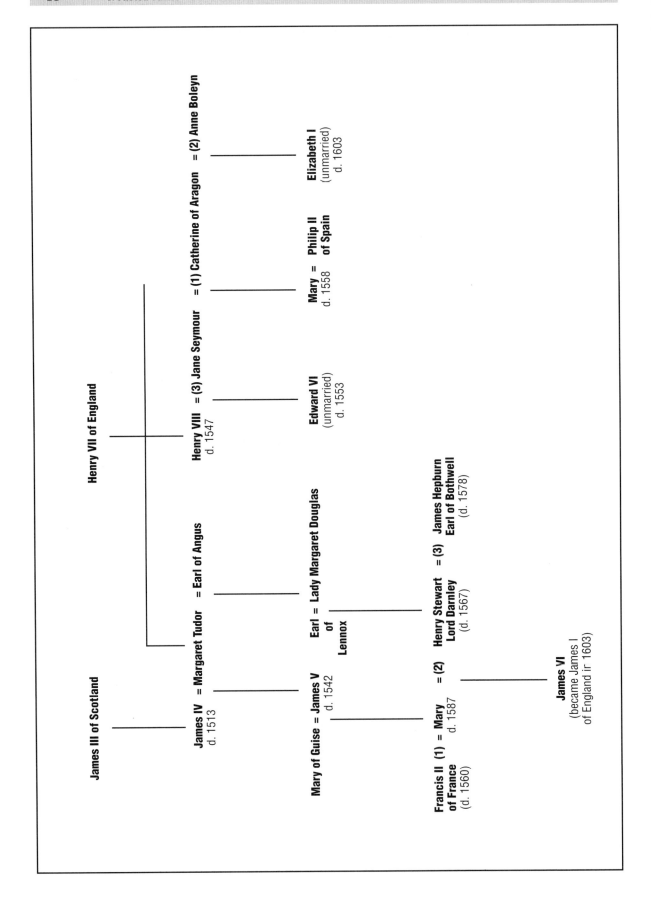

Henry VII of England

James III of Scotland

James IV = **Margaret Tudor** = **Earl of Angus**
d. 1513

Henry VIII = (3) **Jane Seymour** = (1) **Catherine of Aragon** = (2) **Anne Boleyn**
d. 1547

Edward VI
(unmarried)
d. 1553

Mary = **Philip II**
d. 1558 **of Spain**

Elizabeth I
(unmarried)
d. 1603

Mary of Guise = **James V**
d. 1542

Earl = Lady Margaret Douglas
of
Lennox

Francis II (1) = **Mary** = (2)
of France d. 1587
(d. 1560)

Henry Stewart = (3) **James Hepburn**
Lord Darnley **Earl of Bothwell**
(d. 1567) (d. 1578)

James VI
(became James I
of England in 1603)

On 24 April 1558, Mary and Francis married. The ceremony took place in Notre Dame Cathedral in Paris. Mary wore a beautiful white dress, a diamond necklace and a crown of gold. A year later King Henry II died as a result of an accident at a tournament when a splinter from a lance went into his eye. Francis became King of France and Mary became Queen. There were even those who said she should be Queen of England too – indeed the French King had arranged for Mary's royal flag to have the English royal coat of arms added to it.

Mary was, in part, descended from the Tudor family who ruled England. In 1558, Henry VIII's daughter, Elizabeth, became Queen of England. Not only was she a Protestant, and therefore regarded with alarm by the Pope and Catholic rulers, but many Catholics did not accept that she was legally Queen. Her mother, Anne Boleyn, had been Henry VIII's second wife. The King had divorced his first wife but had gone against the Pope's wishes in doing so.

STOP AND THINK

Look at the family tree and explain why Catholics believed Mary was the rightful Queen of England.

Mary was not Queen of France for long. Her husband was small, pale and sickly. In November 1560, he fell ill after a day's hunting. He developed a fever and died on 5 December. His younger brother Charles now became King of France. Mary, at just eighteen years of age, decided the time was right to return to Scotland to rule the country. Great changes had been taking place in her absence. Mary returned to find that the Protestant faith now had strong support among many important people.

The growth of Protestantism

- A number of Scots went to the continent to study Protestant beliefs. They included Patrick Hamilton who studied at Martin Luther's University. He preached in Scotland. In 1528, he was arrested and burned to death as a heretic.
- George Wishart studied in St. Andrews and Switzerland. He became a teacher in Montrose and preached his Protestant beliefs. He was arrested by Cardinal Beaton's men and burned as a heretic. This angered many people.
- Henry VIII and then Somerset helped the Scottish Protestants. Henry encouraged them to kill Cardinal Beaton.
- A group of Scottish Protestants broke into St. Andrews Castle, stabbed Beaton to death and hung his body from the window from which he had watched Wishart burn. They controlled the castle for over a year.
- One of Wishart's followers was a former priest, John Knox. He joined the group at St. Andrews and was captured when French forces took the castle.

John Knox

- For his punishment, Knox spent 18 months as a slave on a French galley. Chained alongside criminals, he helped power the ship by rowing one of its huge oars, being whipped when he was too slow. He then went to Geneva and became interested in John Calvin's beliefs. Calvin believed that only a select group of Christians, chosen by God, would be saved from the torments of hell. He believed in simple services provided in plain churches and in Bible study by everyone.
- An increasing number of influential Scottish lords became Protestants. In 1557 they began to organise themselves, using the name the Lords of the Congregation.
- In 1558, an 82-year-old-Protestant, Walter Myln, was burned as a heretic. This horrified many people.

Under foreign influence: Scotland divided

The Queen Mother, Mary of Guise, became Regent in 1554. She persuaded the Earl of Arran to give up his post as Governor in return for a French dukedom, an income, and positions for several of his family. Frenchmen were given important positions in Scotland, and Mary of Guise placed more taxes on Scottish people. When in 1558 the young Mary married the French heir, Scotland and France were united. Although the French pretended to agree that Scottish laws would be preserved, secret arrangements stated that the Scottish crown would pass to the French if Mary died childless.

From 1553 to 1558 the Catholic Mary Tudor was Queen of England and, like Mary of Guise and her French supporters, wanted to crush Protestantism. When Mary Tudor died, however, on 17 November 1558, her younger half-sister Elizabeth, a Protestant, became Queen – and Scottish Protestants hoped that she would help them. Scots opposed to the French or who disapproved of foreign influence (they were not all Protestants) were increasing in number. The Lords of the Congregation, an organised movement of nobles, had 7 important nobles (such as James Stuart) and 42 lesser lords by 1560. English agents had also for some years been handing out Protestant writings and Bibles in English to encourage the Reformation to spread.

A Protestant Triumph

By 1559 there was strong anti-Catholic feeling throughout Scotland:

◆ FRIARS – members of a Catholic organisation that was devoted to living a poor life and helping the poor. They lived in friaries

- Statements called 'Beggars Summons' were nailed on the doors of friaries, telling FRIARS to leave and give their money to the poor.

- On 11 May 1559 John Knox, newly returned to Scotland, preached such a fiery sermon in St John's Church. Perth, that people rushed from it to burn Catholic religious buildings.

- A growing number of burghs, including Dundee and Perth, declared that they were Protestant.

- There was a revolt against Mary of Guise, with Scots leaders trying to end her authority, although they lacked the power to do so.

- In February 1560 Elizabeth I signed the Treaty of Berwick, agreeing to send English ships and soldiers to Scotland.

- In June 1560 Mary of Guise died.

- In July 1560 the Treaty of Edinburgh was signed – French and English forces agreed to leave Scotland, and the French agreed to drop Mary's claim to Elizabeth's crown.

The Scots Parliament that met in 1560 was controlled by men who sympathised with the Reformation. They agreed to end the power of the Pope over the Church in Scotland and to abolish the religious service of the Latin Mass. Very many Scots were still Catholic, but Queen Mary faced returning to a country where many of the most influential people were now Protestant.

◆ CALVINISTS – Protestants, followers of John Calvin

John Knox and many CALVINIST preachers urged their leaders to go even further. Knox was an influential person and his views included the belief that:

To promote a woman to rule over any nation or city is [offensive] to God. It is a thing most contrary to his revealed will and approved law.

Mary had just lost both her mother and her husband. She was returning to a land divided over religion. She would be surrounded by quarrelsome and violent men who were jealous of each other. Although her close friends, the four Marys, returned from France with her, Mary faced a life that was likely to be lonely. Yet she had still not reached her nineteenth birthday when she landed in her homeland.

STOP AND THINK

Why were the Scots such a divided people at this time?

Practise Your Skills

Answer the questions that follow, using the sources and your knowledge as appropriate.

Source A, from John Knox's account in 1546 of the death of his friend George Wishart, an early Protestant leader:

'**The hangman said "Sir, I pray you forgive me for I am not guilty of your death". Wishart kissed his cheek and said "Lo, here is a token that I forgive thee. Do thine office". Then he was put on a gibbet and hanged and then** burned to powder. When the people saw the tormenting of the innocent they could not hold back piteous mourning and complaining of the innocent lamb's slaughter.'

1 How valuable is this source as an account of Wishart's death? (Evaluate historical sources taking into account origin or purpose and context.)

Source B, from an account by a French visitor to Scotland of events after the Battle of Pinkie:

'English soldiers burned their towns, plundered the low country, took control of all the important places in the Borders and even had the cheek to gallop about, day and night, up to the gates of Edinburgh, charging about the area.'

2 Explain why English forces launched repeated attacks on southern Scotland at this time. (Explain historical developments and events.)

Chapter 2: An overview

- Henry VIII tried to gain control of Scotland through the Treaty of Greenwich which stated that his son Edward would marry Mary.
- The Scottish Parliament was angry with Henry's decision, and they rejected the Treaty. Henry, and then the Duke of Somerset, launched fierce attacks on Scotland, including the English victory at Pinkie.
- Unable to stop these attacks, the Scottish leaders agreed to the Treaty of Haddington with France. Mary was sent to France and eventually married the heir to the French throne. French forces drove away the English.

- Led by Mary of Guise, Queen Mary's mother, French (Catholic) influence grew. Protestant influence was growing too. John Knox was a powerful leader of Scottish Protestant Reformers.
- In 1559, a Scottish rising began against Mary of Guise which, in 1560, was supported by the new Queen of England, Elizabeth. After a period of fighting, the French and English agreed to leave Scotland. Mary of Guise died.
- Protestants now held important positions. In 1560 Parliament secured the place of Protestantism in Scotland by ending the authority of the Pope.

Mary's Rule

Key Points
This chapter deals with:
■ How Mary was received on her return.
■ Her meetings with John Knox.
■ Her dealings with the nobles.
■ Her travels around Scotland.
■ Her marriage to Henry, Lord Darnley.

The Queen's return

On 19 August 1561, the two ships carrying Mary and her followers docked at Leith. They brought not only her servants, three of her uncles and the four Marys, but also a great quantity of luggage, including 60 gowns and 180 items of jewellery. A thick mist covered Leith, and the ship's approach was unseen. Mary's sudden appearance surprised local people. She was taken to the house of a merchant, Andrew Lamb, while messengers rode to Edinburgh. Her journey to the city took place through friendly welcoming crowds, some of whom then gathered at night outside her rooms in Holyrood Palace to entertain her with singing.

Mary as a teenager.

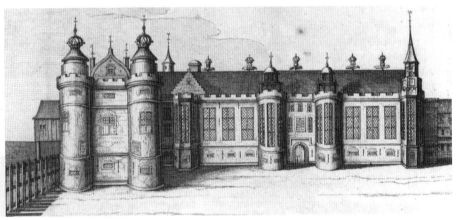

Holyrood Palace where Mary had her private apartments.

Two days later Mary was formally welcomed in Edinburgh. She was carried into the burgh under a canopy of purple velvet fringed with gold. Fifty men dressed in yellow suits with black capes and masks went before her. Dinner, music and entertainments happened afterwards.

There were signs of trouble too. Mary was a Catholic. When it was known that she had gone to her private chapel to hear Mass, an angry crowd began to gather. Mary's Protestant half-brother, James Stuart, had to persuade the people to leave. When she was presented with the keys to the city, she was also, to her annoyance, given a Bible in English and a Protestant service book.

Mary's life at Holyrood

Mary's home was Holyrood Palace which her father had built, and her private apartments were four rooms in the great north tower. Friends and servants, several of whom were French, gathered around her. At night she slept in a huge four-poster bed with curtains around it to keep out the cold. Mary enjoyed riding, hunting, falconry and golf. Her quieter hours were spent gossiping, playing cards or sewing. Above all she loved dancing. A French courtier had already noted:

> *She danced excellently to music on account of her wonderful agility of body, but gracefully and becomingly.*

Sometimes Mary performed in theatrical dances, called masques. These involved performers dressing in elaborate costumes, often as gods, and sometimes women wore men's clothes. There could be well over a hundred guests at the great banquets, where they enjoyed mutton, poultry, venison, hare, pigeon, pheasant and fish. Mary's French cooks brought new recipes to Scotland.

The devotion of her courtiers could be a problem. One of them, a French poet, Pierre de Chatelard, became so infatuated with the Queen that he first tried to hide under her bed at night. He later burst into her bed chamber and had to be forced to leave. This last event was seen to be so serious that the unfortunate poet was tried and executed. His last words were:

> *Adieu, the most beautiful and most cruel princess in the world.*

Controlling the country

Mary was not an experienced ruler, yet she faced the need to control her powerful nobles and, as a Catholic Queen, to avoid being seen as a danger to her Protestant subjects. At first she relied on her Protestant half-brother James Stuart. He was the son of James V and Margaret Erskine, and was twelve years older than Mary. She rewarded his service with the earldom of Moray.

Mary knew she had to be tolerant of the Protestant religion, which she herself did not follow. She did not interfere in the position of Protestantism, made sure the Protestant Church had an income, and agreed that priests were not to say Mass – indeed several priests were prosecuted for this offence. In return, she asked to be allowed to follow her own faith in her private chapel.

For many Protestants this worked well enough, but there were some who were so sure that Catholicism was wrong that they could not accept a Catholic Queen. Their leader was John Knox. From his pulpit in St Giles he denounced Mary's Catholic faith and her whole way of life. When it seemed that Mary might marry a Spanish Catholic, he preached against it and he was especially harsh about her dancing. Knox was an important person, and Mary therefore asked him to meet her. They had several meetings, but if she hoped to win him over, she hoped in vain. Instead she had to listen to his long religious arguments. He even put forth the view that people did not need to obey an 'ungodly' ruler. It was this that most concerned her, for she felt that Knox was trying to turn her subjects against her. He seemed ready to blame her for anything, as in this instance:

> *In 1563 there was a great famine in Scotland. But in the north where Mary had travelled before harvest time, the famine was hardest and many died. Thus did God punish the sins of our wicked Queen; the riotous festivity and huge banquets in the palace and in the country provoked God into this action.*

The Queen took her responsibilities seriously. She went to the meetings of her Privy Council and worked with her capable secretary, William Maitland of Lethington. She placed great importance on travelling around her kingdom. Indeed between 1562 and 1565 she spent two-thirds of her time travelling, and covered well over 1,600 miles. These journeys allowed her subjects to see her and, she hoped, strengthened their loyalty to her. Her travels took her to Aberdeen, Inverness, Perth, Stirling and her palaces at Falkland and Linlithgow. Courtiers, servants and soldiers travelled with her. Often the court stayed at the houses of nobles or wealthy citizens who bore all the costs of the Queen's visit. So spending time in different places actually helped to support and provide for her court.

Mary wept easily, and at one of their meetings Knox reduced his Queen to floods of tears.

On one occasion Mary's travels took her into danger. The Catholic Earl of Huntly and his family, the Gordons, dominated the north east of Scotland. For some years Huntly had administered and benefited from the lands of the vacant earldoms of Mar and Moray. Mary's appointment of James Stuart as Earl of Moray ended this income and made Huntly jealous. When Mary travelled up to Inverness she found Huntly's eldest son there, refusing her entry. When he was finally persuaded to back down, he was arrested and executed by Mary's followers. Huntly gathered his forces and threatened the Queen. Eventually this rebel army met Mary's armed supporters, led by Moray and Maitland of Lethington, at Corrichie. There, on 28 October 1562, Huntly's army was totally defeated. Huntly died soon afterwards, another of his sons was executed, and the family stronghold, Huntly Castle, was sacked.

Military expeditions sometimes involved the Queen herself. Mary was quite prepared to travel with and encourage her army, as events in a few years time were to show.

Marriage

Several European princes were eager to marry the young Scottish Queen. They included the King of Sweden and the Duke of Finland. For some time Mary hoped to marry Don Carlos, the son of the powerful King of Spain, Philip II, but Philip ended this plan when his son suffered serious brain damage in a fall. Elizabeth of England did not wish to see Scotland allied to one of her Catholic enemies. She tried to convince Mary that if she rejected all her Catholic suitors then she might be named as Elizabeth's heir. It was some time before Mary realised that Elizabeth was using her.

Several Scottish nobles, too, had hopes of marrying the Queen. In 1565, during one of her travels around her kingdom, Mary met the man she was to marry. Henry Stewart, Lord Darnley, was a Scottish noble whose father had been living in exile in

England. He was nineteen years old, tall, good-looking, fashionably dressed and fond of hunting, and he had considerable skill in flattering, entertaining and pleasing Mary. He wrote this verse of poetry to her:

> *My hope is you for to obtain*
> *let not my hope be lost in vain*
> *Forget not my pains manifold*
> *Nor my meaning, to you untold*
> *And else with deeds I did you crave*
> *with sweet words I you for to have.*

He was Mary's cousin because his mother was the daughter of Margaret Tudor, widow of James IV, and her second husband. His father, the Earl of Lennox, belonged to a branch of the Stewart family.

However, it was impossible to please some Scottish nobles without angering others. The Hamilton family were not pleased. Mary's half-brother, James, Earl of Moray, was especially angry. The fact that the Earl of Lennox was a Catholic and was allowed to return from exile to Scotland alarmed Protestant lords like the Earl of Morton and Lord Ruthven. Several of them signed an agreement to prevent Darnley marrying Mary.

STOP AND THINK

Why was the choice of Mary's husband so very important?

Mary and Darnley, painted by an unknown artist.

◆ MESSENGERS AT ARMS – uniformed officers who carried out official orders.

Mary was determined to make her own choice. She made Darnley Earl of Ross, and eventually married him at Holyrood on 29 July 1565. Darnley claimed to be a Protestant and left the part of the ceremony when Mass was heard. A lavish banquet and dancing followed. Handfuls of coins were thrown to bystanders. Royal MESSENGERS AT ARMS travelled around Scotland to spread news of the wedding, standing at market crosses blowing loud blasts on horns before shouting the news.

Whatever ordinary people thought, several nobles resented Darnley. When heralds announced to them that Darnley was to have the title of King of Scots, only his father, the Earl of Lennox, cheered. The Earl of Moray especially resented being displaced. He feared that Darnley meant to take away some of his lands and even claimed that there were plots to murder him. Mary heard rumours that Moray planned to kidnap Darnley and ordered him to appear before her. When Moray refused, she declared him an outlaw and gathered an army.

The events that followed are known as the Chaseabout Raid. Moray moved to various places trying to gain support for his small force. He appealed in vain to Elizabeth for English help. Mary pursued him at the head of her army, travelling as far as Dumfries. Moray fled to England without fighting. Mary had acted vigorously, and danger seemed at an end. This episode brought the Queen into contact with another man who was to play a big part in her life – James Hepburn, Earl of Bothwell. He returned to Scotland and joined her campaign, and she made him her lieutenant general since he seemed to offer vigorous and loyal military leadership.

STOP AND THINK

Why was the Earl of Moray so angry about Mary's marriage?

Practise Your Skills

Answer the questions that follow, using the sources and your knowledge as appropriate.

Source A, from the writings of the modern historian, Rosalind Marshall, about Mary's return to Scotland in 1561:

'It seemed that the entire population had turned out to see her. Dull though the weather was, the whole atmosphere had been turned into one of spontaneous rejoicing. ... all who saw her were delighted with her. She was young, beautiful and charming and, elated by the unexpected warmth of her reception, she responded with laughter ... to the crowds that pressed around her.'

Source B, from the writings of John Knox about Mary's return:

'The very face of heaven [at] the time of her arrival did ... speak what comfort was brought into this country with her, that is sorrow, darkness and [false beliefs] for ... the mist was so thick and so dark. The sun was not seen to shine for two days before nor two days after.'

1 In what ways, and for what reasons, do sources A and B differ? (Evaluate historical sources taking account of origin or purpose: a comparison is made between two sources.)

Source C, from the writings of Thomas Randolph, the English ambassador to Scotland in 1562:

'Her journey is painful and marvellous long: the weather extremely foul and cold. On Tuesday she arrived at Old Aberdeen to prepare to enter the new town where she was honourably received with [shows], plays and other [entertainments].'

2 Explain why Mary travelled around Scotland. (Explain historical developments and events.)

Chapter 3: An overview

Mary's return

Mary was welcomed by most Scots and set up court in Holyrood Palace.

Mary's tolerance

She remained Catholic, but left Protestantism alone to flourish. However, she argued with Knox.

Mary's authority

She travelled around her kingdom meeting her subjects and displaying her authority as Queen of Scots. She dealt swiftly with the rebellion of the Earl of Huntly. She accompanied her army on the Chaseabout Raid.

Mary's marriage

She married Henry, Lord Darnley, and made him King of Scots.

Mary's troubles

Knox's followers attacked her beliefs and her way of life. Nobles who disliked Darnley and were jealous of the Lennox family were a constant threat.

Murders, Mysteries and Exile

Key Points
This chapter deals with:
- Mary's problems with Darnley.
- The murder of her servant Rizzio.
- The murder of Darnley.
- Mary's marriage to Bothwell.
- The rising against her, her defeat and imprisonment.
- Her escape, her second defeat and flight to England.

An unhappy marriage

Marriage to Darnley did not bring Mary happiness. He did not take state business seriously. He preferred to wander about Edinburgh with other young men, getting drunk and associating with various women, including prostitutes. Darnley became increasingly angry with his wife because she would not give him the power he believed he should have. Soon after their marriage, he asked for an agreement that should Mary die childless, the children he might have with a second wife would inherit the crown. Mary refused to agree to this. (She was in fact pregnant before the end of the year.) Discontented nobles encouraged Darnley's anger. They included the Douglas family, led by the Earl of Morton, who also gained a surprising new ally – the Earl of Moray.

Moray was living in exile. He feared that the next Scottish Parliament would pass a law taking his lands from him. The Earl was prepared to agree to help Darnley in return for a promise that he could come back to Scotland and keep his land.

A cruel murder

By early 1566, Mary's pregnancy was advancing and she was spending a lot of time indoors. This gave a good deal of influence to those who were close to her. One of these was David Rizzio, an Italian who had become the Queen's secretary. Despite his rather unattractive appearance, Rizzio was entertaining, witty and a skilled musician. The people around Darnley encouraged him to be jealous of Rizzio, even suggesting that the Queen might be having an affair with him. Eventually a plot was laid.

On 9 March the Queen and a group of friends were enjoying a candle-lit supper in a small room in Holyrood when Darnley arrived. A visit from the Queen's husband was most unusual, yet he seemed in a good mood. Then the door burst open and Lord Ruthven, one of the plotters, stood there in full armour, his face a ghastly white. The Queen reported that:

On seeing David Rizzio he declared he wished to speak with him.

Rizzio realised the danger. Ruthven drew a pistol, and followers of Lord Morton rushed in. The Queen later wrote:

L ord Ruthven advanced towards Rizzio who had gone behind my back and the table was knocked over. They then most cruelly took him out of the room and struck him 56 times with daggers and swords.

The murder of Rizzio. His body was thrown downstairs and a porter stole his fine clothes.

When the Provost of Edinburgh arrived outside with a crowd of townspeople, Darnley prevented Mary from reaching the window. Lord Lindsay stopped her screams by threatening to 'cut her into collops' (slices of meat). Darnley defended his own behaviour, arguing that Rizzio had come between him and the Queen. Certainly many nobles resented Rizzio's air of self-importance and his efforts to make them come to him with any requests meant for the Queen. But Mary wept for Rizzio until, drying her eyes, she said:

N o more tears now. I will think upon revenge.

Kirk O'Field

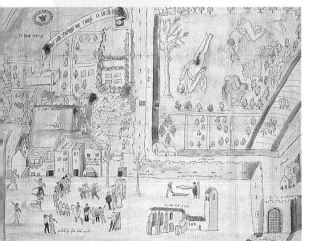

The mysterious murder of Darnley

On 10 February 1567 a terrible murder took place at Kirk O'Field just outside Edinburgh. Darnley, the Queen's husband and his servant, William Taylor, lay dead. An artist of the time drew this sketch (to send to the English government) on which several events are shown. In the top right lie the bodies of Darnley and his servant Taylor. Bottom left is the drawing of a crowd watching the bodies being moved. Bottom right, Taylor's body is being buried. Centre left stand the ruined remains of what had once been a sizeable house. Top left, the infant Prince James, (Mary and Darnley's son born in June 1566) cries out for revenge on his father's murderers. What happened? What caused it to come about? Who was to blame? Was this Mary's revenge?

Countdown to murder

1   After Rizzio's murder, Darnley's courage failed him. He abandoned Morton and the other plotters. He and Mary went from Edinburgh to the greater safety of Dunbar. The Earls of Bothwell and Huntly helped them. They gathered a large army, and Morton and Ruthven had to flee to England. These lords were angry with Darnley.

2   Mary found it convenient to use Darnley. She did not show him any affection or respect. She made peace with Moray and he regarded Darnley with contempt. Mary became increasingly devoted to Bothwell.

3   On 19 June 1566, Mary gave birth to a son, James, in Edinburgh Castle. She feared that Darnley might plot with others to take him. The King of France and Queen Elizabeth of England agreed to be godparents, though they did not come to the actual christening. Darnley seemed increasingly bitter and was drinking a great deal.

4   Morton and his friends were keen to return to Scotland. There were discussions among the lords about how to end Mary's marriage. Mary agreed to pardon the murderers of Rizzio.

5   Darnley became ill. Mary visited him in Glasgow and seemed more sympathetic. As he began to slowly recover, he agreed rather reluctantly, and at the last minute, to travel to Kirk O'Field on the outskirts of Edinburgh and stay there in the old Provost's lodging.

6   At Kirk O'Field he became much stronger. Lord Robert Stuart warned him to leave soon or it would cost him his life.

7   On 9 February 1567 the Queen attended the marriage of a favourite page in Edinburgh, went to Kirk O'Field, then returned to Edinburgh around 10 p.m. to go to a masque held to celebrate the page's wedding. Darnley and his servant, William Taylor, remained at Kirk O'Field, alone.

8   Gunpowder was packed into the cellars of the old Provost's lodging and the house was blown up in the night, with a huge bang.

9   People nearby thought they heard Darnley cry out, 'Pity me kinsmen'. He would only have said this to relatives from the Douglas family.

10   Darnley and Taylor were found lying dead in the orchard by the house, untouched by the explosion and free of stab or gunshot wounds or signs of strangulation.

A foreign ambassador reported what was said about the murders:

> *It was made public that the gunpowder had been laid by the Lords Bothwell and Morton who afterwards pretended to be most active in searching out murderers. They said they were acting for the good of their country and to free the Queen from the misery she suffered at the hands of Darnley.*

The Queen wrote:

> *L*ast night at 2 a.m. the house in which the King was sleeping was blown into the air with such force the whole house was demolished. Gunpowder must have been responsible, but who is to blame? I have no idea. Whoever it is will be harshly punished as a warning to others.

However, she did not mourn Darnley for very long. As we shall see, on 15 May she married Bothwell.

The Earl of Lennox accused Bothwell of the murder of his son. Bothwell was acquitted at the trial in Edinburgh because he filled the city with his armed followers, and Lennox dared not come to press his accusation.

STOP AND THINK

Who killed Darnley? Look for clues in the 'countdown to murder' and suggest an answer.

There is no definite answer to the question of who killed Darnley. Two modern historians have arrived at contrasting conclusions. Rosalind Marshall writes (*Queen of Scots*, 1986):

> Modern scholars incline to the view that many more people than Bothwell plotted the explosion. ... Maitland, Morton, Bothwell and probably Moray and many more agreed that they would kill the husband of the Queen. ... It is much more plausible that she knew nothing.

However, Caroline Bingham writes (*Darnley*, 1995):

> [Mary's] explanation of the murder ... was that the explosion at Kirk O'Field had been intended to kill both her and her husband but her life had been miraculously saved by her departure to attend the masque. However this tale was received with scepticism since the fact that Mary had brought Darnley to Kirk O'Field and departed so opportunely looked more like good management than good fortune or ... divine intervention.

Did Darnley and his servant hear noises, climb out of the house window into the garden, escaping the explosion only to be caught and smothered? It suited men like Moray and Morton to blame Bothwell. They got confessions from men involved with Bothwell, but only by torture. Those who confessed were then executed.

Bothwell and Mary's downfall

In late April 1567, Mary set off for Stirling to see her infant son. On her way back she and her 30 followers were stopped by Bothwell. He had a large troop of armed men with him and no-one dared to resist when he insisted that Mary go with him to

Dunbar. Bothwell was an ambitious man. Although married, he had repeatedly asked the Queen to marry him. Now she was in his power and, according to one of her followers, Bothwell raped Mary.

Mary and Bothwell then went to Edinburgh. On 7 May Bothwell's wife divorced him (for adultery with a servant). Eight days later he married the Queen. The other nobles were furious at this rise in power of a man known for his aggressive and arrogant behaviour. Mary herself soon realised she had made a terrible mistake. Bothwell's behaviour was rough and ill-mannered. Led by the Earls of Morton and Moray, the Lords swore to separate Bothwell from Mary and raised an army. Bothwell and Mary gathered their own supporters and the two armies faced each other at Carberry Hill, near Edinburgh. Morton's troops carried a huge white banner showing the infant James calling for vengeance for his dead father.

It was a hot mid-June day and as time passed the troops became restless – some even drifted away. One of the rebels rode across from the enemy camp. Eventually he persuaded Mary that if she gave up, the rebel lords would be loyal to her, and Bothwell could go free. She was led back to Edinburgh, riding through jeering crowds. Far from giving her loyalty, her captors were determined to end her rule, make the baby James King and organise a regency to rule the country while he was a child. This would give them power and end any danger of punishment for their involvement in Darnley's death.

STOP AND THINK

Were the lords justified in rebelling against Mary?

Discuss with a partner, considering the mysterious death of Darnley and her hurried marriage to Bothwell.

Bothwell tried in vain to gather support. He had to flee the country, and eventually landed in Norway. There he was caught by people to whom he owed money and by the family of a girl whom he had abandoned after an affair. He spent the rest of his life in prison. Bothwell died in 1578, insane, having spent his last days chained to a pillar half his height so that he could never stand upright.

Mary's captivity and escape

Mary was taken to Lochleven Castle on a tiny island in the middle of a lake.

As Mary signed her ABDICATION, she declared she would not be bound by a forced signature. On 29 July 1567, five days after signing, James was crowned King. His uncle the Earl of Moray became Regent.

Mary remained imprisoned for months. Her escape on 2 May 1568 was due to the affection she won from two of her captors and the support she continued to enjoy from others outside the castle. The castle belonged to Sir William Douglas who was the Earl of Morton's cousin and the Earl of Moray's half-brother. But William's brother George fell in love with Mary and planned her escape. He was helped by Willie Douglas, an orphan boy. The plotters arranged for Lord Seton, one of Mary's supporters, and his friends to wait on the bank while Mary escaped. Willie Douglas chained up all the boats except the one they needed. He then got the all-important key to unlock the castle doors in a way later described by the Venetian ambassador:

Lochleven Castle

◆ ABDICATION – to officially give up the throne

*T*he key lay on the table where the Governor took his meals. The Queen planned that a page, when serving his master, would place a napkin on top of the key and then remove both without anyone noticing.

Disguised as a servant, Mary was led out of the castle, rowed across the lake, and galloped off to freedom. George Douglas served her for several more years: Willie Douglas stayed with Mary for the rest of her life. But freedom did not last long. Though the Hamilton family and several earls, bishops and other lords rallied to her, with their men, her army was stopped by a much more experienced force led by Moray. At Langside on 13 May 1568, Mary's badly led army was beaten, and she had to flee. She reached the shores of the Solway Firth and crossed to England in a fishing boat. She was only 25 years old, but was never to see Scotland again.

Practise Your Skills

Answer the questions that follow, using the sources and your knowledge as appropriate.

Source A, from the English ambassador's letter home about Darnley:

'**He is of an insolent temper and thinks that he is never sufficiently honoured. The Queen does everything to oblige him, though he cannot be prevailed upon to yield the smallest thing to please her.**'

1 Describe the problems that her marriage to Darnley caused Mary. (Demonstrate knowledge and understanding of historical developments, events and issues.)

Source B, from Mary's own account of escaping from Scotland:

'**I have endured ninety-two miles across the country without stopping to alight and then I have had to sleep upon the ground and drink sour milk and eat oatmeal and have been three nights like the owls.**'

2 Explain why Mary had to leave Scotland. (Explain historical developments and events.)

Chapter 4: An overview

Mary's Problems

- Her secretary, Rizzio, was murdered by jealous lords helped by Darnley.
- Her husband seemed no help to Mary, and so she relied increasingly on the Earl of Bothwell.

- **Darnley was killed, probably by a group of lords including Morton and Bothwell**

- Mary married Bothwell but he was not popular. Other lords organised themselves against him.
- Faced with an army raised by the lords, Mary surrendered, was taken to Lochleven and was forced to abdicate.
- Mary escaped, raised an army, but was defeated at Langside and fled to England.

Mary's Last Years

Key Points
This chapter deals with:
- Why Mary's arrival in England gave Queen Elizabeth problems.
- Mary's life in exile.
- The events that brought about her execution.

After her escape Mary arrived in the north of England and was taken to Carlisle Castle. She appealed to Elizabeth for help. Elizabeth sent Sir Francis Knollys to interview her. He reported that Mary tended:

> *T*o speak much, to be bold, to be pleasant. She showeth a great desire to be avenged on her enemies … the thing that she most thirsteth after is victory.

STOP AND THINK

Why might Mary's arrival in England be such a problem for Elizabeth?

Elizabeth's problem with Mary

What should Elizabeth do?

- If she helped Mary in Scotland it might end a government there that was pro-English. It suited Elizabeth to have Scotland ruled by men who looked to her for help.

- If she sent Mary back without help she might be imprisoned or even executed. Elizabeth knew Mary was Scotland's rightful Queen as well as her relative.

- If Mary were allowed to live freely in England she might be the focus for Catholic plotters who saw her as the rightful Queen of England.

- If she sent Mary abroad then Catholic rulers there might use her to rally support against Elizabeth.

So … Elizabeth played for time.

In 1568–9 a group of English COMMISSIONERS met at York to hear accusations against Mary. Moray and Morton argued that Mary had plotted with Bothwell to kill Darnley. They sent a silver casket (a box) with eight love letters and a poem in it, which they claimed proved that Mary and Bothwell had been lovers before Darnley

◆ COMMISSIONERS – officials appointed by the ruler or a law court to carry out their instructions

died. These 'casket letters' soon vanished: they may well have been forgeries. The commissioners could not decide if Mary was guilty. But nor could they agree that Moray and Morton were wrong to rebel.

Mary's imprisonment in England

Elizabeth dare not let Mary go free, nor would she meet Mary. Moreover, she became increasingly alarmed by Catholic threats to herself and her country.

- In 1570 the Pope declared that Elizabeth was no longer England's rightful Queen, stating, 'I take away Elizabeth's false claims to the throne. English nobles and subjects are excused all promises, loyalty or obedience to her.'
- On 24 August 1572 French Catholics carried out the 'St. Bartholomew's Day Massacre' killing many hundreds of French Protestants in Paris.
- In 1580 the Pope declared that a Catholic who killed Elizabeth to end the rule of a heretic would not have committed a sin.
- Philip II of Spain, a Catholic and Europe's most powerful ruler, turned increasingly against Elizabeth.

The English Parliament became increasingly worried that Mary was a threat to the safety of the Queen. Shortly before his death, John Knox wrote to Elizabeth urging her to deal with Mary.

Several plots to replace Elizabeth with Mary were formed. In 1569 several leading northern English Catholics planned to free her. They failed, fled to Scotland, and were arrested by Moray. The next plot was organised by Roberto Ridolfi, an Italian banker and agent of the Pope. He hoped to use Spanish troops to free from the Tower of London, not only Mary, but also England's leading Catholic, the Duke of Norfolk. There was even talk of Norfolk marrying Mary. The failure of this plan led to Norfolk's execution. In 1583, the Throckmorton Plot (for a Spanish invasion) failed, and in 1585, Dr Parry's scheme to kill Elizabeth was easily dealt with.

These dangers led Elizabeth to appoint Sir Francis Walsingham to root out plotters. He was a devoted Protestant and a very clever man, skilled in using spies to trap Elizabeth's enemies. He was determined, above all, to trap Mary.

None of the plots directly involved Mary – indeed she said that the thought of Elizabeth's murder horrified her. Yet the plots increased the feeling that a living Mary was a cause of danger. Walsingham searched for evidence that would force Elizabeth to agree to a trial.

Mary's imprisonment

On the move
Mary did not stay in just one castle. She was moved from place to place according to how worried Elizabeth was about plots to free her. Carlisle seemed too near Scotland so she was moved. She lived at Bolton Castle in Yorkshire for a while, but this seemed too near the northern English Catholics and she was moved again. She was moved many times during the 18 years she was imprisoned.

Some comfort
For a while Mary's jailer was George, Earl of Shrewsbury. He allowed her to go riding and hawking, to have visitors and plenty of servants. For some time she stayed in the comfort of Chatsworth House, in Derbyshire. She was allowed to go to Buxton to bathe in the local healing mineral waters. There she met several leading English nobles. She met local people near her place of captivity and gave money to the poor.

Harsher times

As the danger to Elizabeth increased, so Mary's life became harder. She especially hated living in Tutbury Castle, in Gloucestershire, saying, 'The garden is fitter to keep pigs in than to be called a garden. I am in a walled enclosure on top of a hill exposed to all winds and bad weather.' In her later years her jailer was Sir Amyas Paulet, a stern Protestant. He reduced the number of her servants. He would not let her go out or write to anyone except the French ambassador – and even these letters he opened. He also stopped her meeting poor people to give them money.

Passing time

During the 18 years she was imprisoned Mary did a great deal of complicated embroidery. As well as sewing, she read, played cards, and wrote numerous letters. She had pet birds and dogs too. But as time passed and freedom seemed quite impossible to obtain, her health became worse. At times she was quite ill and she suffered a good deal from rheumatism. By the time of her final crisis, when she was 44 years old, Mary seemed almost glad that so weary a life was ending.

The Babington Plot

Walsingham finally got the evidence he needed in 1586. One of his agents, Gilbert Gifford, a former Catholic priest, persuaded Mary that he could arrange secretly to smuggle letters to and from her. They would be hidden in beer barrels. This brought Mary into contact with Sir Anthony Babington. He planned to use foreign aid to release Mary and place her on the English throne. Until now Mary had kept away from any kind of commitment to plotters. But she had just heard that her son, whom she had hoped would rescue her, had signed a treaty of friendship with Elizabeth which did not mention his mother. Against the advice of her secretary, Claud Nau, she dictated a note to Babington agreeing to his plan. It is a sign of her despair that she took such a risk.

This note went straight to Walsingham, who forged an extra section in which 'Mary' asked for the names of the men who would kill Elizabeth. He then resealed it and sent it on to Babington. Babington was arrested and executed. Mary's fate was also sealed because the English Parliament had already voted that she must face execution should there be any further plot against Elizabeth.

The day of 11 August began well for Mary, because her stern jailer, Paulet, allowed her to go out hunting with her two secretaries. But a group of horsemen approached with news that her involvement in the Babington Plot was known.

Mary on trial

Mary's two secretaries were arrested. They were questioned, confessed to Mary's involvement with Babington and were put in prison. Mary was taken to Fotheringhay Castle, in Northamptonshire, a strong building used as a state prison. Her old rooms at Tutbury Castle were searched. Now she had to face trial.

Mary never accepted that she had plotted to kill Elizabeth nor that the court had the right to try a Queen. She declared:

I am myself a Queen ... and the true kinswoman of the Queen of England. I came to England on my cousin's promise of assistance against my enemies and rebel subjects and was at once imprisoned. As an absolute Queen, I cannot submit to orders ... I do not recognise the laws of England.

Londoners rejoiced while Elizabeth wept. There was little sign of real mourning for Mary in Scotland. She was buried at Peterborough Cathedral. In 1612 her son James, who by then was also King of England, had her remains moved and placed in a magnificent tomb in Westminster Abbey.

At first she thought of not even attending the trial, but then learned that she would be condemned in her absence. For two days, 14–15 October, she defended herself. Mary had no one to help her. She was not allowed to call witnesses. She was not permitted to have papers to consult. She defended herself with great dignity, yet in the end the court condemned her. As Mary said to one of her staff:

Did I not tell you this would happen? I knew they would never allow me to live. I was too great an obstacle to their religion.

Mary's execution

Elizabeth had to sign Mary's death warrant. For weeks she could not bring herself to do it. Eventually, on 1 February 1587, a great pile of papers was placed on Elizabeth's desk which she later claimed she signed hurriedly without reading. One of them was the death warrant.

On 7 February Mary learned she was to be executed early the following day. She again declared her innocence and her Catholic faith, and said:

You will do me great good in withdrawing me from this world out of which I am very glad to go.

STOP AND THINK

Why did Elizabeth wait for such a long time before signing Mary's death warrant?

She spent her last hours with her servants. Six of them were allowed to go with her to join a crowd of three hundred who gathered to witness the execution. Mary wore a long black dress over a red petticoat for her final walk to the execution block. The executioner asked her forgiveness, which she gave before kneeling and placing her head on the block to await the blow from the axe. Two strokes were needed to kill her and a third to sever the head which the executioner then lifted. A witness later wrote:

One of the executioners espied her little dog which had crept under her clothes, which could not be got out, but by force, yet afterwards would not depart from the dead body.

Practise Your Skills

Answer the questions that follow, using the sources and your knowledge as appropriate.

Source A, from an English official's report about Mary to Elizabeth's chief minister, 1569:

'I asked her Grace how she passed the time within. She said that all day she worked with her needle. The [many] colours made the work seem less tedious.'

1 Describe the conditions in which Mary lived in prison in England. (Demonstrate knowledge and understanding of historical developments, events and issues.)

Source B, from Mary's letter to Anthony Babington, 1586:

'When everything is prepared and the forces are ready both in this country and abroad, then you must set the six gentlemen to work. Give orders that when the act is done, they get me away from here. At the same time get all your forces in battle order to protect me while we wait for help from abroad.'

2 Explain why the Babington Plot finally led to Mary's execution. (Explain historical developments and events.)

Chapter 5: An overview

Escape to England

1568 Mary escaped to England hoping for Elizabeth's help.

Imprisonment

1569 Elizabeth feared that Mary would be the focus of English Catholic and foreign plots. Mary was not set free. Her prisons varied in comfort.

Catholic plots

Plots by English Catholics began including:

1569 The Northern Catholics
1571 The Ridolfi Plot
1583 The Throckmorton Plot
1585 The Parry Plot
1586 The Babington Plot

Walsingham's spies used these unsuccessful plots to root out enemies. In the last plot they trapped Mary.

Mary's death

1586 Mary had to stand trial in hopeless circumstances. She defended herself bravely.
1587 Mary was executed early in the morning. She died courageously.

Regents and Reformation

Key Points
This chapter deals with:
- The different Regents who ruled while James VI was very young.
- How the Protestant Reformation in Scotland developed.
- James VI's first years as the official ruler and the difficulties he faced.

James as a child

◆ RECENT – a man or woman appointed to rule the country if the monarch was a child (or otherwise incapable of ruling)

The early years of James VI

When James was crowned King in 1567, he was just 13 months old. The crown was so heavy it could not be placed on the infant's head but had to be held over it. Until the age of 19 the King was too young to rule Scotland himself. Nobles acted as REGENTS for him.

The young King was brought up as a Protestant. He was put in the care of a Protestant tutor, George Buchanan, one of the great scholars of the age. He made James study for many hours. James mastered Latin and French, studied history, geography, astronomy and the sciences. His library grew to number 700 books and he never lost his love of learning.

James's tutor was a stern man. The King lived a lonely early life, his father having been murdered and his mother imprisoned in England. He was starved of affection and, in later life, tended to be over-grateful to those who showed him friendship. He was easily charmed and impressed by handsome young men.

His early life was lived in dangerous times. Two of his Regents were murdered and another executed. Nobles and clan chiefs quarrelled and often resorted to violence. A group of MacDonalds, for example, killed their McKenzie enemies by burning down the church where the McKenzies were worshipping. In 1582, James was kidnapped by a group of Protestant lords led by Lord Ruthven (the 'Ruthven Raid'). The lords had been alarmed that James's favourite, Esmé Stewart, his cousin whom he had made Duke of Lennox, was too sympathetic to Catholics. James was rescued in 1583 and he ended Ruthven's power.

It is not surprising that James hated violence. He feared the sight of knives and swords so much that he found it hard to carry out the ceremony of knighting by holding a sword. Sometimes he piled furniture against his bedroom door for fear of attack. He often wore clothes that were thickly padded to protect him in case of a knife attack.

The 'Ruthven Raid' of 1582 also confirmed James's concern about Protestant influence. The General Assembly of the Church liked Ruthven's beliefs, voted in his

The Regents

The Earl of Moray

Mary's half-brother, the Protestant James Stewart, Earl of Moray, became the first Regent. He had to face a very serious war with Mary's supporters (who included Protestants and Catholics) led by the Hamilton family in the West and the Earl of Huntly in the North East. Moray tried to get English help, but Elizabeth was suspicious of men who had deposed a Queen. In January 1570 Moray was killed. He was shot by one of the Hamiltons from a staircase window as he rode through Linlithgow. Mary organised a pension for his killer.

Earl of Lennox

The Earl of Lennox, grandfather of the young King, could not bring peace to Scotland and was killed in a night raid on Stirling where he and his friends were gathered.

Earl of Mar

The Earl of Mar's regency lasted just a year: he died of natural causes, not violence.

The Earl of Morton

James Douglas, Earl of Morton, became Regent in 1572. He was a devoted Protestant and a very active and determined ruler. Morton succeeded in bringing the war with Mary's supporters to an end. In 1573 he made peace with a leading enemy, the Earl of Huntly. His pro-English policies won him military support from Elizabeth. English troops, with cannons, ended the resistance of Mary's last supporters who had been holding Edinburgh Castle. Their leader Kirkaldy of Grange, was executed. The rest of his former enemies still resented him. Morton tried to bring peace to the Borders and to end feuds between nobles. But his taxes were not popular and other nobles

were jealous of him. In 1580 his enemies had him arrested for being involved in Darnley's murder. In 1581 he was executed in Edinburgh Grassmarket by a special beheading machine that he had introduced to Scotland himself.

◆ PRESBYTERIES – Church organisations that supervised the work of several churches in a local area and were made up of ministers and leading men in the congregation

◆ DIVINE RIGHT – the idea that the King had been chosen by God i.e. no one had the right to question his authority

favour and took the chance to set up several PRESBYTERIES. But James wished to keep control of the church – indeed he believed he was a King by 'DIVINE RIGHT', which meant God had chosen him. His enemies called the laws he passed in 1584 the 'Black Acts', because they declared that the Church was to have bishops chosen by the King and that all ministers must accept James's beliefs.

James took personal control of Scotland in 1585. By 1587 he had already shown himself to be skilful and tactful, winning over nobles, avoiding serious conflicts at home and keeping out of foreign wars. His government was endlessly short of money, so gifts from Elizabeth of England, though never enough, were very welcome. Burgh merchants eager for peaceful trade, lawyers keen to see the rule of law, and many folk who were weary of years of conflict, helped his policies to succeed.

Moreover James could look forward to becoming King of England too. In 1586, in return for a treaty of peace and friendship between England and Scotland, Elizabeth named James as her successor and granted him an income. It seemed very unlikely that James would do anything for his mother, and, as we have already seen, her life was now in serious danger.

STOP AND THINK

Why was James so determined to prevent war?

Think about his early life and make a list of possible reasons.

The progress of the Scottish Reformation

In 1560, when Parliament had voted to abolish the service of Mass and the Pope's power in Scotland, many Scots were still Catholics and so was their Queen. The Protestant Church was short of money and ministers – in 1561 only a quarter of parishes had a Protestant Minister or READER (an unqualified person able to read prayers and sermons). Protestants were not even agreed about the sort of Church they wanted to set up. And yet Scotland became a Protestant country.

◆ READER – unqualified person able to read prayers and sermons in Protestant services

Protestants had power

Several leading nobles, like Moray and Morton, were Protestants. Usually most members of Parliament were Protestant. Some nobles and lesser lords formed a powerful organisation, the Lords of the Congregation. This meant that laws were passed against Catholics. A few Catholics were executed for saying Mass. In 1567 a new law was made to say that official positions at court, in burghs, universities and the law, must be held by Protestants. In addition, Elizabeth of England helped Protestants in Scotland.

In contrast, Catholics were not well organised and not well led. Queen Mary accepted the power of the Protestant leaders and James VI was brought up to be a Protestant.

The Protestant Reformation moved slowly

There was no widespread and violent attack on the Catholic Church. Priests and bishops stayed on in Scotland – but were not allowed to carry out religious duties. Three bishops and several priests joined the new Protestant Church. Monasteries were generally left to die off slowly for lack of money, and lack of new monks. Friaries were closed – but friars got pensions. The nobles and laymen who were commendators holding Catholic Church property generally kept it.

Protestantism was attractive

The Protestant style of worship meant that people could be much more involved in worship. The Bible was available in English, not Latin. In 1579 the first Scottish-produced Bible appeared. It cost £40 – a whole year's wages to a craftsman – yet better-off families began to get their own Bibles. The whole congregation took part in saying prayers and singing psalms – whereas Catholic church music had usually been sung by priest and choir alone.

In each Protestant church the members elected Elders every year to help run affairs. This proved to be a popular position.

Money to support the Protestant Church was found

At first the Protestant Church struggled, but Queen Mary provided help. About a third of the income of the Catholic Church was taken over and divided between the monarch and the Protestant Church. The rest remained in the hands of whoever possessed it. After 1572 when a Catholic bishopric fell vacant, the post was not filled so that Protestant ministers could also draw on the money that would have been the bishop's income. The Protestant Church still needed more money, but it had the start that helped it get going. By 1574 most parishes had Protestant ministers except in the Highlands and Borders.

STOP AND THINK

Why did the Protestant cause triumph? What reasons can you find in this section?

What sort of Protestant Church?

During the rest of the period covered by this book, and for many years afterwards, there were differences between Protestants about the kind of Church they wanted to set up.

- Some people wanted to keep archbishops and bishops and have them appointed by the crown. They were happy to see some of the Catholic Church's former wealth stay in private hands. The most important of these people was King James VI.

- Some people wanted to abolish bishoprics. Instead they wanted bodies called 'presbyteries' to take charge of groups of parishes. These presbyteries would be made up of ministers and some church elders. They also wanted control of all of the Catholic Church's former wealth. The most important of these people were John Knox and Andrew Melville.

Knox and his followers

In the period up to 1587, bishops remained. But Knox and his followers produced powerful arguments, especially in *The First Book of Discipline* (1561) where Knox attacked the way Mary had divided the Catholic Church's money, saying:

I see two parts freely given to the devil and the third must be divided between God and the devil.

He believed that the Protestant Church needed far more money for the new churches and other purposes. He believed that the Church had a duty to help poor people. He wanted schools set up in every parish so that everyone could learn to read, write, count, and learn orderly and godly behaviour. Knox also believed that universities should be developed and reformed to produce the ministers and school masters needed. Knox preached regularly in St Giles, in Edinburgh. In 1564, at the age of 50, he married 17-year-old Margaret Stuart. He died in 1572.

Knox's beliefs were carried further by Andrew Melville. He was the son of an Angus laird and a highly intelligent man skilled in Latin, Greek and Hebrew. He studied and taught in several Continental cities. In Geneva he was impressed by the ideas of Theodore Beza who was against any system of bishops. In 1574 Melville came back to Scotland to be Principal of

Glasgow University. In 1580 he moved to St Andrews University and developed it as a centre for training ministers.

Melville became the Church's leading spokesman. Many of his ideas were put forward in *The Second Book of Discipline* (1578). His key ideas described in this book were:

- The positions of archbishops and bishops should be abolished and their duties taken over by presbyteries of ministers and church elders appointed for life.
- The General Assembly should be changed. This body was in overall charge of the Church and included nobles and burgh representatives as well as ministers and elders. Melville wanted it just to consist of ministers and elders.
- Knox and others wanted the local churches, the kirks, to control people's behaviour to improve it. Melville wished to take this much further and be even stricter.
- All the former property of the Catholic Church should go to the new Protestant Church.
- The Church's authority was to be greater than the government's in matters of belief, behaviour and morals. This view troubled King James because it suggested that the Church could say that a ruler was 'ungodly' and that people did not have to obey their ruler.

Life under Protestant rule in Scotland

The fact that Protestants were so much in power in these years did mean that more laws were passed to try to control people's behaviour.

1563   Adultery was made a crime with strict punishments.
1579   There were punishments for 'breaking the Sabbath' by working, travelling, dancing or drinking on a Sunday.
1581   Parliament passed an Act bringing in fines for swearing.

In areas where churches had the support of the people in authority, Melville's followers punished people for drunkenness, failing to attend church, Sabbath breaking, and, above all, for sexual misconduct. Sinners were expected to repent in public and accept various forms of punishment such as standing or kneeling by the church, wearing sackcloth, or being whipped. Since Melville believed that every day should be devoted to God, special holy days like Christmas should not be holidays with bonfires, carol-singing and dancing. Any showy display, such as at weddings, was frowned on, and ministers were expected to wear clothes in dark colours. However, for the moment, this growing list of regulations was not obeyed everywhere.

STOP AND THINK

Why were the Protestants so against display and extravagant celebration?

The Protestant Church was soon strongly established in the burghs. It spread into the Lowland countryside too; but in the Highland area its success was very limited.

Although people living under the Kirk's authority lost holidays (like saints' days) and entertainments (like miracle plays), there were ways in which they made gains. Now they had the chance to share in the running of Church affairs. The Bible and the services were provided in English, a language that most Lowland Scots understood – indeed, the use of Bibles translated in England helped to spread the English language in Scotland.

Kirk ministers were keen to persuade their church members to study the Bible at home. This encouraged the setting up of schools. Attempts were made to encourage and support poor people who could not afford school fees. Melville stressed that church members had a duty to help the poor so that begging could be ended. University education expanded and improved, partly because it needed to produce more church ministers and school teachers. Many members of the Kirk appreciated what it tried to do for their lives.

Practise Your Skills

Answer the questions that follow, using the sources and your knowledge as appropriate.

Source A, from the views of an English visitor on Scottish Protestants in the late sixteenth century:

'They keep no holy days [as holidays] nor acknowledge any saint but St Andrew. Their Sunday exercise is preaching in the morning and persecuting in the afternoon. They hold their noses if you speak of bear baiting, and their ears if you speak of play.'

Source B, from the writings of the modern historian Ian Whyte:

'With the spread of Andrew Melville's ideas there was a sustained attack on many aspects of popular culture, including the celebration of religious festivals, and other Sabbatarianism. In the Calvinist view salvation could only [come] in a society that was consciously godly in its principles. It thus became the business of the church to regulate the lives of everyone.'

1 How far do the views in Source B agree with those in Source A? (Evaluate sources – compare sources.)

Source C, from James Melville's 1581 account of the death of the Earl of Morton:

'He was condemned to be beheaded on a scaffold and that head, which was so clever in worldly affairs and policy and had commanded with such authority and dignity, to be set on a spike upon the highest stone in the tollbooth.'

2 Explain the reasons for the Earl of Morton's downfall. (Explain historical developments and events.)

Chapter 6: An overview

Scotland was divided over

The rule of Regents
Different groups of nobles struggled for power:
- The nobles supporting Mary battled with those opposing her until the fall of Edinburgh Castle, captured with English help.
- The noble who became Regent attracted the hatred of nobles who were his rivals.
- Moray and Lennox were killed, and Morton executed. Feuding among the nobles flourished.

The Reformation
- The Protestant Church gradually increased its control.
- The supporters of Knox and Melville wanted reforms to set up a Church that was free of bishops, and well-funded to help education and the poor.
- Supporters of bishops, and of royal power disagreed.

The rule of James VI
- Had a troubled early life, full of danger including being kidnapped in the 'Ruthven Raid'.
- Would not agree to Melville's ideas and stayed in control of the Church.
- Began to rule sensibly and cautiously to bring peace to his kingdom.

Postscript: Remembering Mary

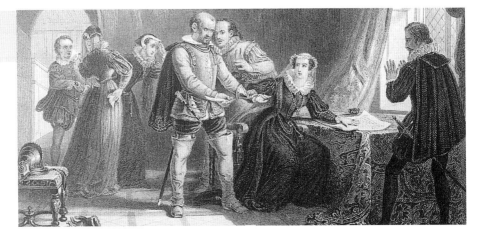

This picture shows Mary being forced to give up her crown. It was painted in 1860 and is only one of many paintings of Mary dating from her lifetime up to the present day. In the Victorian period, when Sir William Allan lived, artists showed the Queen in a very sympathetic and romantic way. Mary has also inspired history books, biographies, poems, plays, films and historical fiction. Many thousands of people visit her tomb at Westminster Abbey every year. Mary's long imprisonment and tragic death seem to stir people's feelings. So do her several romances, which all seemed to end in sadness. She inspired great devotion among some of the people who knew her. She had courage and, when young, great beauty.

Does she deserve to be remembered because she was important? She was Queen for a very short period, in the last part of which she struggled to control her kingdom. She had to accept a form of Christianity in Scotland in which she herself did not believe. The great events of the Reformation were changing Scotland and changing Scottish attitudes to England. James VI's Protestant upbringing made him acceptable to Elizabeth as a person fit to succeed her as ruler of England. This did not unite the two countries, but sharing the same monarch made a big difference to future relationships and events.

Is it possible to see Mary as a Scottish heroine? She grew up in France. It was Scots who drove her out of Scotland. A leading Scot, John Knox, repeatedly denounced her as wicked. Yet according to the American academic Jayne Elizabeth Lewis in her book *Mary Queen of Scots* (1998):

> Her ghost has since captivated many a private imagination … no one
> can venture into England without stumbling across some monument
> to her memory … in Scotland the corridors of Holyrood House all
> seem to lead to Mary's bedroom …

STOP AND THINK

Why do you think there has always been such strong interest in Mary?

Extended Responses

The Intermediate 2 Course requires students to produce an Extended Response. It counts for a quarter of the marks for the whole course. Your Extended Response could come from this course unit.

Always remember to:

- Find a part of the course that especially interests you.

- Work out and discuss a question on this that you believe you could answer.

- Read as much as possible.

- Make organised notes to gather information from which to answer the question. (It will help if you can work out a list of subheadings for your question.)

- See if you can find a few short quotes from historians and from people at the time (primary sources) to copy down.

- Make a plan of how will you answer your question. This plan must not be more than 150 words long. You may take this plan with you when you write out your full answer. It must be sent in with your full answer.

- Set out your plan so that your full answer has a general introductory paragraph, a clear conclusion and, between these, well-organised paragraphs on different parts of the answer. These should have in them the evidence to prove you have good reasons for your views.

How to choose a question

Choose a part of the course in which you are interested and about which it is fairly easy to find more to read.

Some possible questions are listed below:

- Why did the Protestant Reformation succeed in Scotland?

- How important was John Knox in the Reformation?

- Why was Scotland not an easy country to rule?

- Did Mary deserve to be expelled from Scotland?

- Was Mary's execution inevitable?

- How did Protestantism change life in Scotland?

- Did foreign interference have important effects in Scotland?

- Why was Lord Darnley murdered?

A possible plan:
'Did foreign interference have important effects in Scotland at the time of Mary Queen of Scots?'

Introduction

Brief outline of problems in Scotland during Mary's childhood.
Quarrelling groups call for outside help – England and France especially keen for control.

English Interference – before Mary's rule

Treaty of Greenwich: Scots cancel Treaty.
English attacks: Battle of Pinkie.
English agents help the spread of Protestantism.

French Interference

Treaty of Haddington: French forces drive the English out of Scotland.
Marriage deal with the French – Mary leaves for France.
Mary of Guise becomes Regent – spread of French influence

English Interference – during Mary's rule

England becomes a refuge for unpopular nobles.
English aid is given to certain Protestants.
Elizabeth tries to influence Mary's marriage.

English Interference – after Mary's rule

English forces help Morton to defeat Mary's supporters.
Further English backing for Protestants.
Elizabeth makes James her heir in return for his loyalty.
The English imprison and eventually execute Mary.

Conclusion

Summarise key moments when foreign interference was decisive in events taking place in Scotland.

Glossary

ABDICATION to officially give up the throne

BURGESSES important men in the burghs

BURGHS larger place often local centres for merchants and craftsmen

CALVINISTS Protestants, followers of John Calvin

COMMENDATOR protector of a church or abbey who had control of its income

COMMISSIONERS officials appointed by the ruler or a law court to carry out their instructions

DEACON leader of a craftsman's guild

DIVINE RIGHT the idea that the King had been chosen by God i.e. no one had the right to question his authority

FREEMAN a man who enjoyed all the rights and privileges of living in a burgh

FRIARS members of a Catholic organisation that was devoted to living a poor life and helping the poor. They lived in friaries

HERETICS people who believed religious ideas that were dangerously wrong

LAYMEN people who were not trained as priests or ministers

LUTHERANS followers of the German Protestant Reformer Martin Luther

MESSENGERS AT ARMS uniformed officers who carried out official orders.

PLURALIST someone holding several church posts at one time

PRESBYTERIES Church organisations that supervised the work of several churches in a local area and were made up of ministers and leading men in the congregation

READER unqualified person able to read prayers and sermons in Protestant services

REFORMATION The name given to the split between Catholics and those who followed the ideas of reformers like Martin Luther (Protestants)

REGENT a man or woman appointed to rule the country if the monarch was a child (or otherwise incapable of ruling)

RIG mound of soil wide enough for a plough to go down its length

TOWNSHIPS places larger than a village but smaller and more rural than a burgh

WRIGHTS men who made things from wood or metal, e.g. cartwright and shipwright

Index